Data: Kids, Cats, and Ads

STATISTICS

TERC

Investigations in Number, Data, and Space®

Dale Seymour Publications®

Menlo Park, California

The *Investigations* curriculum was developed at TERC (formerly
Technical Education Research Centers) in collaboration with Kent State
University and the State University of New York at Buffalo. The work was
supported in part by National Science Foundation Grant No. ESI-9050210.
TERC is a nonprofit company working to improve mathematics and science
education. TERC is located at 2067 Massachusetts Avenue, Cambridge,
MA 02140.

This project was supported, in part,
by the
National Science Foundation
Opinions expressed are those of the authors
and not necessarily those of the Foundation

Managing Editor: Catherine Anderson
Series Editor: Beverly Cory
Manuscript Editor: Karen Becker
ESL Consultant: Nancy Sokol Green
Production/Manufacturing Director: Janet Yearian
Production/Manufacturing Coordinator: Barbara Atmore
Design Manager: Jeff Kelly
Design: Don Taka
Illustrations: DJ Simison, Carl Yoshihara
Composition: Archetype Book Composition

This book is published by Dale Seymour Publications®, an imprint of
Addison Wesley Longman, Inc.

Dale Seymour Publications
2725 Sand Hill Road
Menlo Park, CA 94025
Customer Service: 800-872-1100

Order number DS47060
ISBN 1-57232-813-4
1 2 3 4 5 6 7 8 9 10-ML-01 00 99 98 97

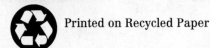

Printed on Recycled Paper

Contents

*Repeated-use sheet

Collecting Data on Balancing

For the balancing test, follow this procedure.

■ Person is allowed to get comfortably balanced on one foot before closing eyes.

■ Timing starts when person closes eyes and says "go."

■ Person can wiggle in place, but not hop or spin. Some part of the foot on the floor must always touch the floor.

■ Foot that is up can't touch the floor or a wall or piece of furniture.

■ Four things can end the test:

Person puts foot down.

Person opens eyes.

Person hops or touches an object for balance.

Person balances for 3 minutes.

■ Person gets one practice trial for each foot.

■ If the person is still balancing at 3 minutes, stop the test and record 3 minutes as the time.

When you are collecting data, be sure to have your eyes on the clock or watch before the person says "go." Right after each test, record two things:

The length of time

Which foot the person balanced on

To the Family

How Long Do Adults Balance?

Session 1

Math Content
Collecting, recording, and making predictions about data

Materials
Student Sheets 1 and 2
Pencil

In class, we have been collecting data about how long we can stand on one foot with our eyes closed. For homework, your child will collect data about how long one or more adults can stand on one foot, for both right and left feet. Remind your child to use the instructions on Student Sheet 1 to guide the data collection, and to record findings on Student Sheet 2.

After collecting the data, your child will write two or more predictions about it. For example, on the basis of the information collected, does she or he think adults will balance, in general, a longer or shorter time than the students in the class? Will there be a difference between left foot and right foot for adult balancers? Who will be the overall longest and shortest balancers? We will explore these questions back in class, with data students will have collected at home and at school.

How Long Do Adults Balance?

How long can adults balance on each foot with their eyes closed? Test two or more adults. Record your findings. Follow the same rules you used at school. The person can practice first, one practice only, on each foot. Remember that 3 minutes is the longest time you can record.

Name of adult	Balance time on right foot	Balance time on left foot

Do you think the adults will be different from you and your classmates? How might they be different? Write two predictions.

1.

2.

To the Family

How Long Do Adults Balance?

Session 1

Math Content
Collecting, recording, and making predictions about data

Materials
Student Sheets 1 and 2
Pencil

In class, we have been collecting data about how long we can stand on one foot with our eyes closed. For homework, your child will collect data about how long one or more adults can stand on one foot, for both right and left feet. Remind your child to use the instructions on Student Sheet 1 to guide the data collection, and to record findings on Student Sheet 2.

After collecting the data, your child will write two or more predictions about it. For example, on the basis of the information collected, does she or he think adults will balance, in general, a longer or shorter time than the students in the class? Will there be a difference between left foot and right foot for adult balancers? Who will be the overall longest and shortest balancers? We will explore these questions back in class, with data students will have collected at home and at school.

Student and Adult Balancers

0 _____

Student Balancing Time on Right Foot

0 _____

Student Balancing Time on Left Foot

0 _____

Adult Balancing Time on Right Foot

0 _____

Adult Balancing Time on Left Foot

To the Family

Comparing Adults and Students

Sessions 2–3

Math Content
Comparing data sets

Materials
Student Sheet 3 (completed)
Student Sheet 5 (begun in class)
Pencil

In class, students have been looking at many aspects of data on adult and student balancing skills, to begin comparing the two groups. For homework, your child will continue on Student Sheet 5 the comparison chart started in school, making two to four statements comparing how long adults and students can stand on one foot.

In order to compare the data on adult and student balancing times, your child may use characteristics such as where more of the data fall, where the largest chunk of data is, what the range of the data is, or where the halfway point (median) falls. Some of the comparison statements might support adults as better balancers, while others might support students.

Who Are Better Balancers?

These statements compare students' balancing data with adults' data. Read each statement. Decide who are better balancers, according to that statement, and write *adults* or *students* in the blank. Write a reason for your answer.

1. Almost $\frac{3}{4}$ of the students balanced for 30 seconds or more, but only $\frac{1}{2}$ of the adults did. _____

2. While $\frac{2}{3}$ of the adults are above 45 seconds, only $\frac{1}{2}$ of the students are above 45 seconds. _____

3. The median for students is 40 seconds, and it's only 30 seconds for adults. _____

4. The students had the lowest score (2 seconds), and they had a larger fraction of scores under 10 seconds. Only $\frac{1}{20}$ of the adults did less than 10 seconds, but $\frac{1}{8}$ of the students did less than 10 seconds. _____

5. Two students balanced more than 1 minute, and no adults did. Also, the top $\frac{1}{4}$ of students scored 50 seconds or more, and the top $\frac{1}{4}$ of adults scored only 40 seconds or more. _____

6. Choose one of the statements above. Make two line plots—one for adults and one for students—that fit the statement. You can use the back of this sheet.

To the Family

Who Are Better Balancers?

Sessions 2–3

Math Content
Comparing data sets

Materials
Student Sheet 4
Pencil

In class, we have been investigating whether fifth graders or adults are better balancers. For homework, your child will complete Student Sheet 4, which makes five statements that compare adult and student balancing data for unseen data sets. After reading each statement, your child will decide who are better balancers, according to that statement. Your child will write *adults* or *students* in the blank and a reason for each answer.

After completing the first five statements, your child will choose one of the five statements and make two line plots—one for adults and one for students—that could fit the statement. Your child may find it helpful to talk through with you ways of thinking about this problem. You might ask such questions as, How many students do you want to have on your line plot? What would 3/4 of that be? Where would you place those on the line plot? How many adults do you want to have? What would 1/2 of that be? Where would you place them on the line plot? Note that your child can choose how many students and how many adults to have in the data set.

Comparing Adults and Students

Continue the comparison chart you started in class. Make two
to four statements comparing how long adults and students
can stand on one foot.

© Dale Seymour Publications®   **9**

To the Family

Comparing Adults and Students

Sessions 2–3

Math Content
Comparing data sets

Materials
Student Sheet 3 (completed)
Student Sheet 5 (begun in class)
Pencil

In class, students have been looking at many aspects of data on adult and student balancing skills, to begin comparing the two groups. For homework, your child will continue on Student Sheet 5 the comparison chart started in school, making two to four statements comparing how long adults and students can stand on one foot.

In order to compare the data on adult and student balancing times, your child may use characteristics such as where more of the data fall, where the largest chunk of data is, what the range of the data is, or where the halfway point (median) falls. Some of the comparison statements might support adults as better balancers, while others might support students.

Mystery Balancers Data

Mystery Balancers A

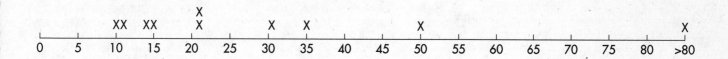

Mystery Balancers B

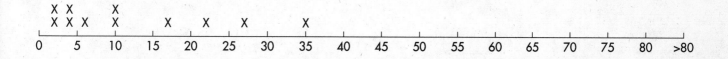

Mystery Balancers C

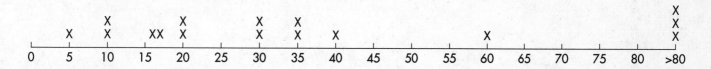

Mystery Balancers D

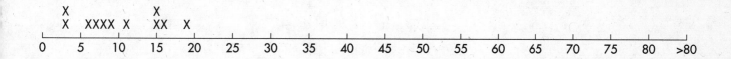

Writing About the Mystery Balancers

Circle the letter of your mystery data: A   B   C   D

Write a report that answers these questions:

- How are your mystery balancers similar to the students in your class? How are they different?

- Is your class better or worse at balancing than your mystery balancers? Or is there no clear "better" group? Give reasons for your answer.

- Which group of mystery balancers do you think you have? Why? If you think two groups are equally likely, name the groups and tell why.

Remember to make statements based on the data.

The Mystery Groups

Gymnasts, ages 9–20

Karate students, ages 16–49

First and second graders, ages 6–8

People over 50

Lady Jane Grey

Gender: female
Age: 4 years
Weight: 8.5 pounds
Body length: 19 inches
Tail length: 11 inches
Fur color: gray
Eye color: yellow
Pad color: gray

Peau de Soie

Gender: female
Age: 15 years
Weight: 7 pounds
Body length: 16 inches
Tail length: 13 inches
Fur color: orange,
              black, and
              white
Eye color: green
Pad color: pink

Other: Peau de Soie means "skin of silk" in French; her nickname is Peau (rhymes with *go*).

Mittens

Gender: female
Age: 14 years
Weight: 10.5 pounds
Body length: 17 inches
Tail length: 11 inches
Fur color: orange and
               white
Eye color: yellow
Pad color: pink

Other: Mittens has six
toes on each foot.

Tigger

Gender: female
Age: 4 years
Weight: 8 pounds
Body length: 17 inches
Tail length: 10 inches
Fur color: orange,
               black,
               and white
Eye color: yellow
Pad color: brown

Weary

Gender:	male
Age:	8 years
Weight:	15 pounds
Body length:	17 inches
Tail length:	12 inches
Fur color:	black and white
Eye color:	green
Pad color:	pink

Ravena

Gender:	female
Age:	6 years
Weight:	14 pounds
Body length:	23 inches
Tail length:	12 inches
Fur color:	orange, black, gold, and white
Eye color:	yellow
Pad color:	pink and black

Lady

Gender:	female
Age:	10 years
Weight:	8.5 pounds
Body length:	17 inches
Tail length:	13 inches
Fur color:	gray, brown, and white stripes
Eye color:	yellow
Pad color:	black

Wally

Gender:	male
Age:	5 years
Weight:	10 pounds
Body length:	18 inches
Tail length:	12 inches
Fur color:	black and white
Eye color:	green
Pad color:	pink and black

Other: Wally is the brother of Peebles.

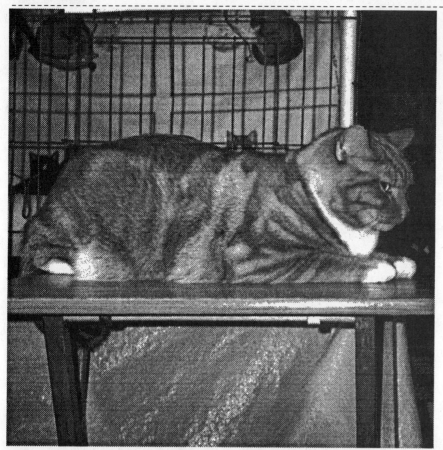

Oddfuzz

Gender:	male
Age:	5 years
Weight:	18 pounds
Body length:	21 inches
Tail length:	9 inches
Fur color:	orange and white
Eye color:	yellow
Pad color:	pink

Melissa

Gender:	female
Age:	8 years
Weight:	11 pounds
Body length:	21 inches
Tail length:	11 inches
Fur color:	white, black, and orange
Eye color:	yellow
Pad color:	pink

Peebles

Gender:	female
Age:	5 years
Weight:	9 pounds
Body length:	17 inches
Tail length:	11 inches
Fur color:	gray
Eye color:	green
Pad color:	black

Other: Peebles is Wally's sister.

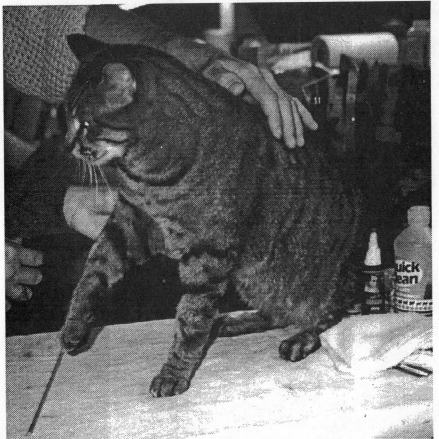

K.C.

Gender:	male
Age:	5 years
Weight:	16 pounds
Body length:	24 inches
Tail length:	12 inches
Fur color:	brown and black stripes, some white
Eye color:	yellow
Pad color:	black

Pepper

Gender:	male
Age:	2 years
Weight:	12 pounds
Body length:	17 inches
Tail length:	9 inches
Fur color:	orange
Eye color:	yellow
Pad color:	pink

Other: Pepper was known as an escape artist at the animal shelter where he was living.

Strawberry

Gender:	female
Age:	16 years
Weight:	14.5 pounds
Body length:	21 inches
Tail length:	10 inches
Fur color:	gray, brown, and white stripes
Eye color:	green
Pad color:	black

Alexander

Gender: male
Age: 18 years
Weight: 11 pounds
Body length: 21 inches
Tail length: 11 inches
Fur color: brown and
                     black stripes,
                     some white
Eye color: green
Pad color: black

Other: Alex's favorite foods are vanilla ice cream and bacon, which he will steal off the table.

Misty

Gender: male
Age: 1 year
Weight: 9 pounds
Body length: 18 inches
Tail length: 11 inches
Fur color: gray, white,
                     and black
Eye color: green
Pad color: pink and
                     black

George

Gender:	male
Age:	12 years
Weight:	14.5 pounds
Body length:	21 inches
Tail length:	13 inches
Fur color:	black and white
Eye color:	green
Pad color:	black

Diva

Gender:	female
Age:	3.5 years
Weight:	11 pounds
Body length:	20 inches
Tail length:	12 inches
Fur color:	gray, black, brown stripes with white patches
Eye color:	green
Pad color:	pink

Gray Kitty

Gender: female
Age: 3 years
Weight: 9 pounds
Body length: 15 inches
Tail length: 8.5 inches
Fur color: gray
Eye color: green
Pad color: gray

Other: Gray Kitty was living at an animal shelter.

Tomodachi Joto

Gender: male
Age: 1 year
Weight: 6.5 pounds
Body length: 14 inches
Tail length: 1.5 inches
Fur color: white and red
Eye color: yellow
Pad color: pink

Other: Tomodachi Joto means "best friend" in Japanese. Nicknamed Joto, he is a Japanese bobtail cat.

Harmony

Gender: male
Age: 3 years
Weight: 12 pounds
Body length: 24 inches
Tail length: 11 inches
Fur color: black
Eye color: yellow
Pad color: black

Augustus

Gender: male
Age: 2 years
Weight: 10 pounds
Body length: 21 inches
Tail length: 11 inches
Fur color: black and
             white
Eye color: yellow,
             green, blue
Pad color: pink and
             black

Other: Augustus, Gus for short, is a long-haired cat. He was found as a stray.

Charcoal

Gender:	male
Age:	11 years
Weight:	12 pounds
Body length:	21 inches
Tail length:	13 inches
Fur color:	black and white
Eye color:	yellow
Pad color:	black

Other: Charcoal has big feet.

Cleopatra

Gender:	female
Age:	4 years
Weight:	7 pounds
Body length:	18 inches
Tail length:	9 inches
Fur color:	black and white
Eye color:	yellow
Pad color:	pink

Collecting Cat Data

Cat's Name		
Gender	Age (years)	Weight (pounds)
Body length (inches)		Tail length (inches)
Fur color	Eye color	Pad color
Other		

Cat's Name		
Gender	Age (years)	Weight (pounds)
Body length (inches)		Tail length (inches)
Fur color	Eye color	Pad color
Other		

To the Family

Collecting Cat Data

Session 1

Math Content
Gathering data to enlarge a sample

Materials
Student Sheet 8
Pencil

In class, we have been sorting and organizing data about cats. For homework, your child will collect more cat data from a cat at home or from a neighbor's or a friend's cat. Your child will use Student Sheet 8 to record the cat's name, gender, age, weight, body length, tail length, fur color, eye color, and pad color. The section "Other" is for recording general comments about anything interesting about the cat.

Remind your child to ask permission from the cat's owner and to find someone to help take measurements. If your child is allergic to cats or afraid of them, someone else can take the measurements while your child writes down the data.

Collecting Cat Data

Cat's Name		
Gender	Age (years)	Weight (pounds)
Body length (inches)		Tail length (inches)
Fur color	Eye color	Pad color
Other		

Cat's Name		
Gender	Age (years)	Weight (pounds)
Body length (inches)		Tail length (inches)
Fur color	Eye color	Pad color
Other		

To the Family

Collecting Cat Data

Session 1

Math Content
Gathering data to enlarge a sample

Materials
Student Sheet 8
Pencil

In class, we have been sorting and organizing data about cats. For homework, your child will collect more cat data from a cat at home or from a neighbor's or a friend's cat. Your child will use Student Sheet 8 to record the cat's name, gender, age, weight, body length, tail length, fur color, eye color, and pad color. The section "Other" is for recording general comments about anything interesting about the cat.

Remind your child to ask permission from the cat's owner and to find someone to help take measurements. If your child is allergic to cats or afraid of them, someone else can take the measurements while your child writes down the data.

The Digits Game

Use the digits 0, 7, 8, 3, 1. You may also use a decimal point.

1. Make a number as close as possible to 1,000. Keep a record of your calculations.

2. Now make a number as close as possible to 500.

3. Make a number as close as possible to 100.

4. Make a number as close as possible to 10,000.

What strategies did you use?

To the Family

The Digits Game

Session 1

Math Content
Estimating and exploring place value

Materials
Student Sheet 9
Pencil

In this game, your child will use a set of digits to make numbers as close as possible to a target number. Remind your child to keep a record of the calculations, and then to write down the strategies used.

You and your child may want to play the game with a different random set of digits, making a number as close as possible to 1000, to 500, to 100, and finally to 10,000.

Variations on the Digits Game

Use the digits 7, 3, 5, and 2 to make addition problems.

1. Make a problem using two 2-digit numbers with a sum as close as possible to 100. Keep a record of your calculations.

2. Use the same digits to make a problem using one 3-digit and one 1-digit number with a sum as close as possible to 500.

3. Make another such problem with a sum as close as possible to 100.

What strategies did you use?

To the Family

Variations on the Digits Game

Session 2

Math Content
Estimating and exploring place value

Materials
Student Sheet 10
Pencil

In this game, your child will use a set of digits to make addition problems, in order to get as close as possible to a target number. Note that this time your child is instructed to make numbers with specified numbers of digits. Remind your child to keep a record of the calculations, and then to write down the strategies used.

Finding Familiar Fractions

During class, write down the questions. Fill in the numbers of people who answered *yes* and *no,* and the total number in your class today. Do the rest for homework. Use either Data Strips or numerical reasoning to find familiar fractions.

Question _____

Answer	Number who answered	Total in class	Fraction who answered	Familiar fraction
Yes				
No				

Question _____

Answer	Number who answered	Total in class	Fraction who answered	Familiar fraction
Yes				
No				

Question _____

Answer	Number who answered	Total in class	Fraction who answered	Familiar fraction
Yes				
No				

To the Family

Finding Familiar Fractions

Session 1

Math Content

Converting data fractions to familiar fractions

Materials

Student Sheet 11
Data Strips
Pencil

In class, we have been collecting data on questions that have two possible answers, and changing these data fractions to familiar fractions. For homework, your child will continue this process, converting data fractions about class data on Student Sheet 11 to familiar fractions. Your child can use either Data Strips or numerical reasoning to find familiar fractions.

If a calculator is available, your child may also want to use it to find decimals and percents for each data fraction.

DATA STRIPS

51

To the Family

Finding Familiar Fractions

Session 1

Math Content
Converting data fractions to familiar fractions

Materials
Student Sheet 11
Data Strips
Pencil

In class, we have been collecting data on questions that have two possible answers, and changing these data fractions to familiar fractions. For homework, your child will continue this process, converting data fractions about class data on Student Sheet 11 to familiar fractions. Your child can use either Data Strips or numerical reasoning to find familiar fractions.

If a calculator is available, your child may also want to use it to find decimals and percents for each data fraction.

Small-Group Sampling

1. Question

2.

Results of small-group sample	
Response	Number of students

3.

Prediction for the whole class, based on sample		
Response	Number of students	Fraction of class

Give a reason for your prediction.

4.

Prediction for the whole class, based on sample		
Response	Number of students	Fraction of class

5. Compare your sample results to the population results. Tell how your small group was similar to or different from the whole class.

Surveys in the News

Find an article in a newspaper or magazine that reports on a survey in which only a sample of a population was questioned. The article must be one that you can understand and explain.

After reading the article, write a paragraph telling:

■ what the survey tried to find out;

■ what the sample was (some news reports do not include details about the sample).

_____

_____

_____

_____

_____

_____

_____

_____

_____

_____

_____

_____

_____

_____

_____

_____

57

To the Family

Surveys in the News

Sessions 2–3

Math Content
Making the link with surveys and sampling in the news

Materials
Student Sheet 13
Pencil
Newspapers or magazines

In class, we have been learning about samples and surveys. For homework, your child will find an article in a newspaper or magazine that reports on a survey in which only a sample of a population was questioned. The article must be one that your child can understand and explain. After reading the article, your child will write a paragraph telling:

- what the survey tried to find out

- what the sample was, if it is reported in the article (some news reports do not include details about the sample)

Meals and Chores Survey

---

1. When your family eats dinner, do you all eat together at the same time?

   yes   sometimes   no

---

2. Do you watch television while you are eating dinner?

   yes   sometimes   no

---

3. What's your favorite meal of the day—breakfast, lunch, or dinner?

   breakfast   lunch   dinner

---

4. Do you get to choose what you eat for dinner?

   yes   sometimes   no

---

5. Do you help set the table?

   yes   sometimes   no

---

6. Do you help cook?

   yes   sometimes   no

---

7. If you had a choice of cooking dinner, setting the table, or cleaning the dishes, which would you choose?

   cook dinner   set table   clean dishes

Questions are from a national survey, "America's Children Talk About Family Time, Values, and Chores," sponsored in 1994 by the Massachusetts Mutual Life Insurance Co.

Survey Results

Responses	National sample	Our class

1. When your family eats dinner, do you all eat together at the same time?

Responses	National sample	Our class
yes	82%	
sometimes	8%	
no	9%	

2. Do you watch television while you are eating dinner?

Responses	National sample	Our class
yes	29%	
sometimes	19%	
no	53%	

3. What's your favorite meal of the day—breakfast, lunch, or dinner?

Responses	National sample	Our class
breakfast	24%	
lunch	33%	
dinner	43%	

4. Do you get to choose what you eat for dinner?

Responses	National sample	Our class
yes	27%	
sometimes	34%	
no	40%	

5. Do you help set the table?

Responses	National sample	Our class
yes	57%	
sometimes	19%	
no	24%	

6. Do you help cook?

Responses	National sample	Our class
yes	26%	
sometimes	37%	
no	37%	

7. If you had a choice of cooking dinner, setting the table, or cleaning the dishes, which would you choose?

Responses	National sample	Our class
cook dinner	37%	
set table	44%	
clean dishes	18%	

Data (rounded to nearest percent) from "America's Children Talk About Family Time, Values, and Chores," 1994, Massachusetts Mutual Life Insurance Co.

To the Family

Meals and Chores Survey Results
Session 4

Math Content
Comparing the data from a sample to the data in a larger population

Materials
Student Sheet 15
Student Sheet 16
Pencil

In class, we have been investigating how our class is like or unlike a larger sample of 8- to 12-year-olds who participated in a national survey on meals and chores. For homework, your child will write about one of our questions about the meals and chores data, including the following points:

- How were our class results the same as or different from the national survey results? Which of these similarities and differences surprised you?

- What could be the reasons for the differences?

- According to the data, is our class a representative sample of the national survey group? Why or why not?

Meals and Chores Survey Results

Write about how your results on the Meals and Chores Survey compared with the national results. Include the following points in your writing:

■ How were our class results the same as or different from the national survey results? Which of these similarities and differences surprised you?

■ What could be reasons for the differences?

■ According to the data, is our class a representative sample of the national survey group? Why or why not?

_____

_____

_____

_____

_____

_____

_____

_____

_____

_____

_____

_____

_____

_____

_____

_____

To the Family

Meals and Chores Survey Results

Session 4

Math Content
Comparing the data from a sample to the data in a larger population

Materials
Student Sheet 15
Student Sheet 16
Pencil

In class, we have been investigating how our class is like or unlike a larger sample of 8- to 12-year-olds who participated in a national survey on meals and chores. For homework, your child will write about one of our questions about the meals and chores data, including the following points:

- How were our class results the same as or different from the national survey results? Which of these similarities and differences surprised you?

- What could be the reasons for the differences?

- According to the data, is our class a representative sample of the national survey group? Why or why not?

Fractions of Newspaper Pages

Choose a page of a newspaper. (Be sure *not* to choose a page that has no ads, is half ads, or is all ads.)

Write a report on what fraction of the newspaper page is ads. Be sure to include the following:

1. name of the paper

2. the page number

3. fraction of the page that is ads

4. fraction of the page that is not ads

5. an explanation of how you figured out the fractions, using words or pictures or both

To the Family

Fractions of Newspaper Pages

Session 1

Math Content
Determining fractions of a whole

Materials
Student Sheet 17
Newspaper
Pencil

In class, we have been using a variety of strategies to find the fraction of a newspaper page that is made up of ads. For homework, your child will choose a page of a newspaper and report the fraction that is made up of ads. Your child's strategies may include any of a number developed in the class (for example, counting the columns and then figuring out how many column-equivalents are ads; cutting out the ads from a page, combining them, and seeing how much area they cover). Your child can explain the strategies used in words, pictures, or both.

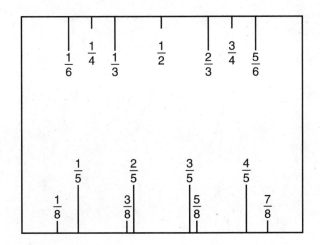

$\frac{1}{6}$ $\frac{1}{4}$ $\frac{1}{3}$ $\frac{1}{2}$ $\frac{2}{3}$ $\frac{3}{4}$ $\frac{5}{6}$

$\frac{1}{5}$ $\frac{2}{5}$ $\frac{3}{5}$ $\frac{4}{5}$

$\frac{1}{8}$ $\frac{3}{8}$ $\frac{5}{8}$ $\frac{7}{8}$

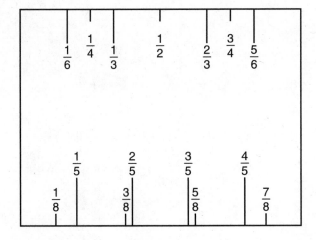

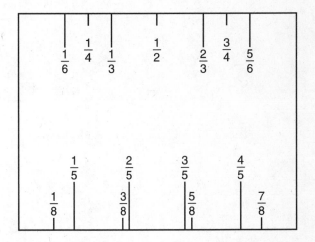

Investigation 4 • Resource
Data: Kids, Cats, and Ads

RECORDING STRIPS

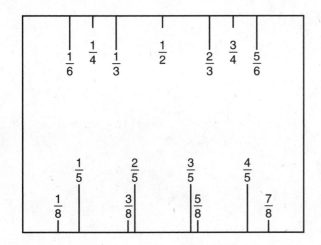

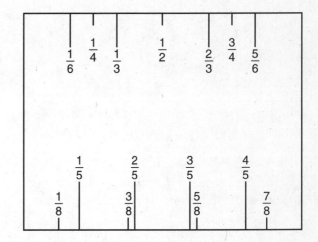

Each box contains fraction markings:

$\frac{1}{6}$ $\frac{1}{4}$ $\frac{1}{3}$ $\frac{1}{2}$ $\frac{2}{3}$ $\frac{3}{4}$ $\frac{5}{6}$

$\frac{1}{5}$ $\frac{2}{5}$ $\frac{3}{5}$ $\frac{4}{5}$

$\frac{1}{8}$ $\frac{3}{8}$ $\frac{5}{8}$ $\frac{7}{8}$

Danger on the Playground

A survey of playground injuries in the United States was done in 1994. Each year 170,000 children are seriously injured on playgrounds. The survey involved 443 playgrounds in 22 states. The researchers defined an injury as anything serious enough that the person had to go to the emergency room. They found these problems:

- In 92% of the playgrounds, the surfaces under equipment were not soft enough. Three-fourths of all injuries are caused by falls. Many of these falls cause head injuries, which can be very serious.

- In 57% of the playgrounds, the climbers and slides were too high—over 10 feet tall. Slides account for about 30% of all playground injuries. Mostly, children fall from the top or sides of the slide.

- Climbers account for 41% of injuries to school children. Many of these injuries involve broken bones.

- In 76% of playgrounds, the swings were too close to each other and to other equipment. About 28% of injuries are caused by swings.

- A serious cause of injuries to young children is getting their heads stuck in equipment. The survey found that 55% of the playgrounds had equipment on which children could get their heads stuck between the rungs.

- About 40% of all playground injuries involve children 6 to 8 years old. Another 40% involve preschool children. About 20% involve children older than 8.

Reference: "Playing It Safe: A Second Nationwide Safety Survey of Public Playgrounds," U.S. Public Interest Research Group and Consumer Federation of America, May 1994.

Practicing the Survey Questions

Ask someone at home to interview you, using the survey questions we wrote in class.

What was it like to answer the questions?

_____

_____

_____

_____

_____

Now interview one or more people yourself.

Write how well you think the questions worked, and suggest how to make them better.

_____

_____

_____

_____

_____

_____

_____

_____

_____

_____

To the Family

Practicing the Survey Questions

Session 1

Math Content
Refining survey questions

Materials
Student Sheet 19
Copy of survey questions
Pencil

In class, students have been considering how safe our school playground is, and they have formulated survey questions they want to ask about injuries. In preparation for actually collecting data, your child will try out the survey questions to see what it's like to answer the questions and how well they work. Your child will first interview one or more people outside of school, and then write an assessment of the questions and make suggestions for making them better.

How to Play the Digits Game

Materials: Numeral Cards (with Wild Cards removed)
Digits Game Score Sheet for each player

Players: 2 or 3

How to Play

1. Decide on the target number to use.

   Example: The target is 1000.

2. Deal the Numeral Cards. Deal out one more card than there are digits in the target.

   Example: The target has four digits, so you deal out five cards: 3, 8, 0, 1, and 5.

3. Players use the numerals on the cards to make a number as close as possible to the target.

   Example: You can use 3, 8, 0, 1, and 5 to make 1035, 853, or other numbers.

4. Write the target and the number you made on your score sheet. Find and record the difference between them.

   Example: 1000 − 853 = 147. The difference is your score.

5. When everyone has finished, compare answers. Which number is closest to the target? Is it possible to make a number even closer?

   Example: Player A made 853. Player B made 1305. Who is closer? Can you make a number with these digits that is even closer to 1000?

6. For the next round, mix up all the cards and deal a new set.

7. After three rounds, total your scores. Lowest total wins.

Digits Game Score Sheet

For each round you play, record the target number and the
closest number you can make with your digits. Put the larger
one first. Then, find and record the difference between them.

Game 1 target: _____   Difference

Round 1: _____ – _____ = _____

Round 2: _____ – _____ = _____

Round 3: _____ – _____ = _____

Total score: _____

Game 2 target: _____   Difference

Round 1: _____ – _____ = _____

Round 2: _____ – _____ = _____

Round 3: _____ – _____ = _____

Total score: _____

Game 3 target: _____   Difference

Round 1: _____ – _____ = _____

Round 2: _____ – _____ = _____

Round 3: _____ – _____ = _____

Total score: _____

Digits Game Score Sheet

For each round you play, record the target number and the closest number you can make with your digits. Put the larger one first. Then, find and record the difference between them.

Game 1 target: _____   Difference

Round 1: _____ – _____ = _____

Round 2: _____ – _____ = _____

Round 3: _____ – _____ = _____

Total score: _____

Game 2 target: _____   Difference

Round 1: _____ – _____ = _____

Round 2: _____ – _____ = _____

Round 3: _____ – _____ = _____

Total score: _____

Game 3 target: _____   Difference

Round 1: _____ – _____ = _____

Round 2: _____ – _____ = _____

Round 3: _____ – _____ = _____

Total score: _____

79

Digits Game Score Sheet

For each round you play, record the target number and the closest number you can make with your digits. Put the larger one first. Then, find and record the difference between them.

Game 1 target: _____   Difference

Round 1: _____ – _____ = _____

Round 2: _____ – _____ = _____

Round 3: _____ – _____ = _____

Total score: _____

Game 2 target: _____   Difference

Round 1: _____ – _____ = _____

Round 2: _____ – _____ = _____

Round 3: _____ – _____ = _____

Total score: _____

Game 3 target: _____   Difference

Round 1: _____ – _____ = _____

Round 2: _____ – _____ = _____

Round 3: _____ – _____ = _____

Total score: _____

Digits Game Score Sheet

For each round you play, record the target number and the closest number you can make with your digits. Put the larger one first. Then, find and record the difference between them.

Game 1 target: _____   Difference

Round 1: _____ – _____ = _____

Round 2: _____ – _____ = _____

Round 3: _____ – _____ = _____

Total score: _____

Game 2 target: _____   Difference

Round 1: _____ – _____ = _____

Round 2: _____ – _____ = _____

Round 3: _____ – _____ = _____

Total score: _____

Game 3 target: _____   Difference

Round 1: _____ – _____ = _____

Round 2: _____ – _____ = _____

Round 3: _____ – _____ = _____

Total score: _____

Digits Game Score Sheet

For each round you play, record the target number and the closest number you can make with your digits. Put the larger one first. Then, find and record the difference between them.

Game 1 target: _____   Difference

Round 1: _____ – _____ = _____

Round 2: _____ – _____ = _____

Round 3: _____ – _____ = _____

Total score: _____

Game 2 target: _____   Difference

Round 1: _____ – _____ = _____

Round 2: _____ – _____ = _____

Round 3: _____ – _____ = _____

Total score: _____

Game 3 target: _____   Difference

Round 1: _____ – _____ = _____

Round 2: _____ – _____ = _____

Round 3: _____ – _____ = _____

Total score: _____

Digits Game Score Sheet

For each round you play, record the target number and the
closest number you can make with your digits. Put the larger
one first. Then, find and record the difference between them.

Game 1 target: _____   Difference

Round 1: _____ – _____ = _____

Round 2: _____ – _____ = _____

Round 3: _____ – _____ = _____

Total score: _____

Game 2 target: _____   Difference

Round 1: _____ – _____ = _____

Round 2: _____ – _____ = _____

Round 3: _____ – _____ = _____

Total score: _____

Game 3 target: _____   Difference

Round 1: _____ – _____ = _____

Round 2: _____ – _____ = _____

Round 3: _____ – _____ = _____

Total score: _____

0	0	1	1
0	0	1	1
2	2	3	3
2	2	3	3

Practice Page
Data: Kids, Cats, and Ads

4	4	5	5
4	4	5	5
<u>6</u>	<u>6</u>	7	7
<u>6</u>	<u>6</u>	7	7

Practice Page
Data: Kids, Cats, and Ads

8	8	9	9
8	8	9	9
WILD CARD	**WILD CARD**		
WILD CARD	**WILD CARD**		

Practice Page
Data: Kids, Cats, and Ads

Practice Page A

Fill in the numbers you say if you start at 1000 and count down by each counting number.

Count down by 10	Count down by 25	Count down by 50	Count down by 250	Count down by _____ (your choice)
1000	1000	1000	1000	1000
_____	_____	_____	_____	_____
_____	_____	_____	_____	_____
_____	_____	_____	_____	_____
_____	_____	_____	_____	_____
_____	_____	_____	_____	_____
_____	_____	_____	_____	_____
_____	_____	_____	_____	_____
_____	_____	_____	_____	_____
_____	_____	_____	_____	_____
_____	_____	_____	_____	_____
_____	_____	_____	_____	_____

Practice Page
Data: Kids, Cats, and Ads

Practice Page B

Fill in the numbers you say if you start at 3 and count up by each counting number.

Count up by 5	Count up by 10	Count up by 50	Count up by 250	Count up by _____ (your choice)
3	3	3	3	3
_____	_____	_____	_____	_____
_____	_____	_____	_____	_____
_____	_____	_____	_____	_____
_____	_____	_____	_____	_____
_____	_____	_____	_____	_____
_____	_____	_____	_____	_____
_____	_____	_____	_____	_____
_____	_____	_____	_____	_____
_____	_____	_____	_____	_____
_____	_____	_____	_____	_____
_____	_____	_____	_____	_____

Practice Page
Data: Kids, Cats, and Ads

Practice Page C

Fill in the numbers you say if you start at 25 and count up by
each counting number.

Count up by 5	Count up by 10	Count up by 50	Count up by 250	Count up by _____ (your choice)
25	25	25	25	25
_____	_____	_____	_____	_____
_____	_____	_____	_____	_____
_____	_____	_____	_____	_____
_____	_____	_____	_____	_____
_____	_____	_____	_____	_____
_____	_____	_____	_____	_____
_____	_____	_____	_____	_____
_____	_____	_____	_____	_____
_____	_____	_____	_____	_____
_____	_____	_____	_____	_____
_____	_____	_____	_____	_____
_____	_____	_____	_____	_____

Practice Page D

For each problem, show how you found your solution.

Suppose there is a new coin called the pentapod. A pentapod is worth 55 cents.

1. How many pentapods are in 3 dollars?

2. How many pentapods are in 7 dollars?

3. How many pentapods are in 20 dollars?

Practice Page E

For each problem, show how you found your solution.

Suppose there is a new coin called the hexafin. A hexafin is worth 36 cents.

1. How many hexafins are in 6 dollars?

2. How many hexafins are in 36 dollars?

3. Will 42 hexafins be enough to buy 4 movie tickets that cost $4.50 each?